GOAT FARM ROAD

POEMS FROM THE ADIRONDACKS

poems by

CATHERINE NORR

Finishing Line Press
Georgetown, Kentucky

GOAT FARM ROAD

POEMS FROM THE ADIRONDACKS

ACKNOWLEDGMENTS

I am most grateful for my life-companion, Dave Schriver, for his constant loving
support, stellar common sense, encouragement and input, and for making it possible
to live "off-grid" at our wonderful Adirondack home.

Gratitude to my long-standing poetry group members, both present and past, for
their spot-on critiques, suggestions and celebrations of creative endeavors.

Continuous thanks for family and friends, particularly Chris and Carol, whose
artistic talents and sharing inspire and nourish me. My children, John and Becky,
Joseph and Becca and the younger family members, Robin, Lee, Jocelyn and Nathan,
are unceasing sources of renewal and optimism.

Thanks to Finishing Line Press, all the editors and staff, for making it possible for this
collection to become a framed work that can be shared.

Publisher: Leah Huete de Maines
Editor: Christen Kincaid
Cover Art: David Schriver
Author Photo: Chris Smither
Cover Design: Elizabeth Maines McCleavy

Order online: www.finishinglinepress.com
also available on amazon.com

Author inquiries and mail orders:
Finishing Line Press
PO Box 1626
Georgetown, Kentucky 40324
USA

Contents

*Go placidly amid the noise and haste
and remember what peace there may be in silence*

Max Ehrmann, excerpt from "Desiderata"

On the Road to Mountain Cabin

walking is best
along the rutted road

awareness alters as you pass through the veil
between noise and silence

even as beech leaves rustle
and chicadees flutter

the tangible quiet thickens
to a surrounding quilted cloud

tracks and markings left behind whisper
history of neighbors
beaver rabbit bear deer

Beyond the Chain

that marks a private way
    past the plowed
        dirt town road

lies a rocky logging trail
        more a dry riverbed than a road

a sandy patch
    then a steep hill
        calls for lower gear

birch and beech
    stretch tall and skinny
        reach for thin sunlight

bend over
    burdened with spring sleet
        form a tunnel that hides the sky

New World

Once I came upon two
tiny snapping turtles
crawling out their broken shells
climbing out of the dirt

On a busy spot of the road
tire tracks close to the fragile nest
mere one-inch hole spared

With breast-strokes
they clawed up and out
miniature green heads stretched
on taut rubbery necks

They headed for the lake
over grass-blades twice their size
over leaves and twigs
stiff with October frost

Spring Back Home Is:

When dandelions are blooming
      yellow among the green
and goldfinch pour song
      over branches of a cherry-tree
When doves pick at seed in the grass
      and pebbles in gravel drive
When the buzz-saw of a hummingbird
      whizzes by to feed
Wood thrush melodies haunt the forest
      and a woodpecker taps a hollow tree
Baby salamanders and toads
      zig-zag across the ground
      a chorus of frogs sounds from the lake
When wind ambles through tops of hemlock
      and brushes across our deck
Deep breaths come easy

At the Cabin

October breeze—
after leaves are swept
clear from the deck
a gust brings down another
burst of crackling color

October breeze—
warm scent of wood-smoke—
mountain ash & maple,
aroma of fresh-cut cedar

October breeze—
sounds of hammer
saw and drill
tap of the
Black-backed woodpecker
and rustle of dry-leaf trees

In Praise of Disposal—a limerick

There once was a house full of Things
Collectables, trinkets and rings
      Photos, papers and more
      All strewn on the floor
We'll sing while we're recycling

We start with boxes of files
Then move on to dishes and tiles
      We sort and we clean
      Till no tchotchkes are seen
Then sit with our Cheshire Cat smiles

Late August

Past the summer solstice
      each morning dew is dense
            on grass and panes

Harvest hangs heavy on stalks
      I sit lazy and indifferent

More family and friends are gone
      long lives that now seem brief

My thoughts even now turn
      to cold winds that will blow
            ice and snow against my door

November Birthday

I move more slowly now
A quiet corner with good light beckons
My bed is more inviting each year

Most leaves have fallen
yet buds already swell on branches
that will bloom next spring
Tight winter nights squeeze my breath

After autumn riots of yellows and reds
snow-shapes now smooth imperfections
like the finest cream
meant to preserve endless youth

Goat Farm Road

is so far off the main highway
that a GPS shows it only as
leave the road—
a gray line trailing through solid green
dead-ending around a narrow body of blue

so the Meerkat Pest-Control guy
drives his van up and down the dirt road
to find his assigned address
but what numbers exist
don't follow a pattern—
as randomly picked as trees
fallen in the latest windstorm

a resident driving a tractor
hails the driver and chats
reveals to the frustrated tech
riddles of the baffling lane
beyond electronics and print-outs

my pathway too often is unclear
till I bump into my next guide
or glimpse a signpost
in the tangled underbrush
along the road

Uprooted

Nature is wielding her wily ways
to snare us into some quiet-time
reflecting light-rays upon old stumbling blocks
"dissolve the suckers" she says
winking and turning the page of one of her folktales
believe-you-me the time is coming when your mind
won't grip and your cryptic answers won't hold
then you're gonna want that soul of yours to know
what it's about now   what it's all about

Haiku

Low-flying heron
Crosses the length of the lake
Its mate follows close

Tin roof amplifies
Raindrops from hemlock and birch
Distant Barred Owl hoots

On Lily Lake Road
Porcupine plods as we near
He speeds to a trot

Wood-thrush melody
Rap-tap of hammer on wood
Woodpecker tap too

On window-ledge nest
Baby phoebe open beaks
Mama-bird hustles

Line of gold edged clouds
Sun sinks behind blossoming trees

Late spring multiple gardeners
Like too many chefs
Debate pruning

Fresh-picked blueberries
Our picnic becomes a feast
Highlight of summer

Burst of blueberry—
Tongue rejoices

Stillness on the lake
Bird-shadow crosses surface
Squirrel chirrup

White clouds scuttle across blue after hail

Madder and Other Reds

Sunday after the biopsy we drive mountain roads
stopping for breakfast at a country café.

It would be another week to wait for results;
autumn foliage our distraction for today.

A dazzling array as we travel valley and hill,
bright yellows dotting hedgerows,
dark evergreen, random tangerine.

The highlight is a stately maple
centered in an emerald field
boasting a revelry of reds—
a madder variety,
carmine and scarlet, crimson and cardinal,
chili-pepper, fire-brick, cinnabar and blood.

Autumn Nap

On branches above me
    crisp leaves shake and quiver
        "B'bye! B'bye!" they wave
    as the wind whips
first one leaf then another
    and another detach
        sail off, spin away
          "This is it!" they murmur

My eyes close, I nap and dream
    of falling and flight
and wake to naked branches
    dark against a violet sky

Words in the Middle of the Night

taking shape over my head

hovering like hummingbirds

perch briefly

sip nectar

dart away

Seedling Reflects

I sing a homesick blues
while waiting for a place
I've known always
during dry sleep
self-portrait under cover
as in a mirror
or in a dream

a peculiar internal dynamism
urges—desire? thirst?

I push through layers of grit
push up through the dark

there's a strong outer pull
felt not seen—an invitation
from the moist warm
a heady-high
above this density

below—shell of myself
brown and crumbling
my upper stretch green
a springtime yellow-green,
and tender, so tender

Birch Tree Peeling—a nine-Tanka meditation

1.
strip of birch tree
hangs down midway on the trunk
it blows in the wind
movement caught my attention
stops when wind ceases blowing

2.
movement caught my eye
narrow skin of birch tree
clings midway along the trunk
the papery strip hangs still
wind generates its dancing

3.
when will it drop off
this papery strip of birch
it clings to the trunk
by one end of its dangle
The ants mind their own business

4.
on ancient birch tree
thin piece of bark dangles loose
the strip is silent
as wind blows it to and fro
while the leaves rustle, rustle

5.
this long narrow strip
on trunk of an old round birch
hangs twelve inches long straight down
other bark peelings
are wide and curling inward

6.
swaying in the breeze
strip of peeling birch skin
clings to the live tree
gouges and scars make dark shapes
against the light gray tree bark

7.
peeling bit of birch
one small part of such huge tree
a mere tiny thread
how it dances with the wind
twirls and brushes against trunk

8.
at this time and place
this simple ragged strip of bark
might be unnoticed
but for prolonged view
bringing attention to small

9.
rings of bark on tree
smooth and tight and uniform
except one loose one
changes pattern—caught my eye
becomes a dancing figure

Positive Results

cancer—the biopsy positive
"is it real?"... "but I feel fine..."
not someone else this time

sudden thrust (trusting) into grinding gears
medical procedures, tests in prep for others
grateful for modern treatments
but moreover discomfort and dread

a new vocabulary moves to the foreground
personal, filled with imaginings
"lumpectomy"& "radiation" (make that a double)
later "endometrial" and "hysterectomy"
and the fearsome what-if—"metastasize"
(take pills to reduce the risk, manage side-effects)
will "survivor" be added to the list?

surgery is best...sleeping an anesthesia deep
wake rested, minus parts you don't need anyway
hold-your-breath as each follow-up proves,
so far, that negative is positive

Twilight Sensation

stories told aloud hold me spellbound
dry textbooks leave me wishing for more

come gather 'round a campfire at dusk
smoke blocking the forest from view

in the telling dreams and memories
slip and shift
sometimes vivid, often blurred

challenged by another's story
my version scatters
like dandelion wishes

In Times of Extraordinary Sight

Birds flying above
are fish under-sea
and we
swim deeper still

And if in meditation
we rise up
to its surface
beyond choppy waves
our eyes behold
an unfamiliar shore
where golden pathways
lead inland to
yet unknown

Others have heard and
observed such scenes
in quiet solitude
internal melodies
and dreams speak
wisdom beyond
natural boundaries

Integral

once blended in greenly among the crowd
the leaves transform
to autumn ripe from inside-out
display their true colors
flamboyant, clear, solid red, yellow, brown
or mottled, dark age-spots dotting multi-hued skins
the same chill wind blows them all down
a colorful collage onto welcoming ground

Catherine Norr, nee Smither, (nickname "Kit") grew up in New Orleans, Louisiana. She and her twin brother, Chris Smither, sang together, sometimes in a trio, during Junior High and High School years.

After Alcee Fortier High School, Norr received a B.A. from Newcomb College, Tulane University, with a French major and minors in Education, Spanish and Studio Art., Norr and husband Stephen, lived in Honolulu, HI where their daughter was born. Their son was born in Rochester, NY.

Norr has held a variety of jobs, including some years as owner/operator of Norr's Ark Pizza and Hicks & McCarthy's (Pittsford, NY), assistant manager at Borders Bookstore (Rochester, NY), teaching French at Saratoga Springs Waldorf School, and singer-songwriter, performing at various venues in Hawaii and New York State.

Catherine shares home, an off-grid cabin in the Adirondacks, with her partner, David Schriver, and their dynamic cat, Marti. Winter is spent in the Verde Valley area of Arizona. Favorite pastimes when not writing, reading or visiting friends & family, are gardening & yard work, quilting & fabric-art, drawing, painting and traveling.